NOON

ALSO BY PHILIP ROWLAND

together still (Hub Editions, 2004)
where rungs were (Noon Press, 2007)
someone one once ran away with (Longhouse, 2009)
before music (Red Moon Press, 2012)
Something Other Than Other (Isobar Press, 2016)

AS EDITOR

Haiku in English: The First Hundred Years (Norton, 2013;
with Jim Kacian & Allan Burns)

NOON

AN ANTHOLOGY OF SHORT POEMS

edited by

PHILIP ROWLAND

ISOBAR
PRESS

Published in 2019 by

Isobar Press
Sakura 2-21-23-202, Setagaya-ku,
Tokyo 156-0053, Japan
&
14 Isokon Flats, Lawn Road,
London NW3 2XD, United Kingdom

https://isobarpress.com

ISBN 978-4-907359-26-3

CONTENTS

INTRODUCTION

This anthology, unlike those which gather work from a variety of sources, draws its contents from a single journal, the thirteen issues of NOON: *journal of the short poem* that have appeared to date: 2004–9 in print, 2014–17 online. NOON is very much a personal project: as I am the sole editor, the work included in each issue, and now this anthology, inevitably reflects my own preferences and preoccupations. Naturally, then, this book does not set out to offer a comprehensive representation of 'the contemporary short poem'; it is simply, as the subtitle states, an anthology of short poems. On the other hand, the contents are more various than most anthologies of short poetry, which tend to be devoted to particular movements or genres, such as haiku. The anthology closely reflects the journal not only in this combination of stylistic variety and personal perspective, but also in format and editorial approach. A fuller introduction to NOON, the journal, may therefore be helpful.

Issues 1–7 were published in limited editions of two hundred copies, hand-bound in Tokyo in traditional Japanese style. More recent issues have appeared online, following the example of the print issues in length (usually seventy to eighty pages) and layout, with a poem, however short, per page. This has not only given – especially in physical book-form – each poem the space to 'breathe'; the poem must also, so to speak, warrant the page. In this way the journal's format has helped open the question: how much can these poems of very few words do, individually and collectively? The challenge is one of concision – but also connection, for each issue is meant to form a sequence of poems, short enough to be read at a single sitting. (To heighten the sense of flow and focus on the writing itself, in print issues contributors' names appeared only in an index, rather than on the poem-pages themselves.)

Likewise, the arrangement of poems in this anthology has been a crucial consideration: they have been carefully juxtaposed throughout. Thus it is not simply a 'best-of' collection, but rather a new configuration of selected poems – a retrospective special issue, effectively. Given the scarcity of the print issues and the 'virtual' form of the later ones, the general aim has been to provide a representative sample of poems from the journal in a more readily available book, offering, it is hoped, a distinctive and wide-ranging selection of contemporary short poetry.

This, then, is much more an anthology of poems than of poets; hence the decision to arrange the contents creatively rather than alphabetically by author. The ultimate goal was not the fullest possible representation of each author, but cohesion (without loss of variety or individuality) among the selections. A number of poems that I'd have liked to include were left out, eventually, to maintain a smooth yet stimulating flow. Editing an anthology inevitably involves difficult choices and reluctant omissions; one could even argue, as did Laura Riding and Robert Graves in their provocative *Pamphlet Against Anthologies* (1928), that anthologies uproot poems from their contexts, imposing misleading categories upon them. But in the approach taken here, I have tried to make the most of these limitations, through meaningful, often playful, juxtaposition and sequencing of the poems, to produce a newly distinctive body of work that is relatively unconstrained by narrow genre-definitions. The result is a *renga*-like chain of over two hundred poems by almost half as many poets. This 'collectiveness' reflects my assumption that the shorter the poem, the greater the importance of context; and many of the poems in this book are, indeed, *really* short.

Which raises the basic question: how short is 'short'? The focus in NOON is on poems shorter than fourteen lines, with the exception of particularly 'skinny' or expansively spaced (but verbally spare) ones. This is largely, of course, to stay out of sonnet territory, though occasionally it has seemed fitting to include particularly pithy or minimalist sonnets (Jim Kacian's 'Sonnet for Philip Glass' on page 107 being a striking instance). Many of the poems, however, fall well below this line-limit, with haiku and minimal poems (sometimes as short as one line, even one or two words) being featured for their particular openness and concision.

Indeed, one of my reasons for starting the journal was that I wanted to read good haiku more often alongside and 'in conversation with' other varieties of innovative short poetry – to explore new kinds of poetic community, rather than to reinforce existing ones. One of the pleasures of editing the journal, and now the anthology, has therefore been to find and foreground connection, sometimes surprising kinship, between quite different poems, often by poets who would not usually be found in the same publication. This may have the effect of dissolving, to some extent, preconceived ideas of distinct or opposed 'schools' of writing: the experimental as opposed to the traditional or pastoral, for example. On the other hand, there are clusters of poems in this anthology by poets with shared histories: in North American haiku, in the innovative British poetry scene, in collaborative writing projects, in acknowledged debts to other poets, and so on. These groupings will seem to reflect more 'natural' lines of tradition and development.

While first publication of most of the poems was in NOON,

occasionally the journal featured rarely printed or newly translated poems. This is reflected by the inclusion, here, of two of Morris Cox's *45 Untitled Poems*, which had only been published in an edition of fifty copies from his own Gogmagog Press in 1969 before a selection was reprinted in the first issue of the journal. Richard Gilbert's and Itō Yuki's translations of Japanese anti-war haiku from the late 1930s, and Patrick Donnelly's and Steven Miller's translations of *waka* on Buddhist themes from centuries earlier, add further elements of historical interest and may suggest lines of continuity with the contemporary poems that comprise most of this anthology.

In these ways, I have sought to be inclusive without being merely eclectic, and to present, in this anthology, as in each issue of the journal, a nuanced arrangement of poems that creates a sense of quasi-collaborative authorship. At the same time, of course, the anthology is meant to point beyond itself, to contributors' individual bodies of work. I have therefore appended a list of those authors' collections in which poems first published in NOON, and included in this anthology, later appeared.

I am grateful to all contributors for their cooperation in this project; likewise, to readers whose responses to the issues helped motivate me to continue the journal, which will resume after the publication of this book. In particular, I would like to thank John Levy, the journal's closest reader and most frequent correspondent over the years, who has also provided fine cover photos for the online issues. I am also very grateful to Isobar's publisher Paul Rossiter for bringing a clear eye to the project and helping to resolve a number of sticking-points in the editing process. It is particularly fitting that this book is being published by Isobar Press, with which NOON shares an outlook, not only in publishing out of Tokyo, but also (in line with the meteorological metaphor suggested by the press's name) in having 'no defining stylistic agenda', while at the same time hoping 'to publish poets whose writing – wherever it may be situated on the stylistic map – is working at equivalently high poetic pressure'.

PHILIP ROWLAND
Tokyo, 22 April 2019

NOON

JOHN MARTONE

you
look up

from
planting

bulbs
into
fall's

new
spaces

I build a stone wall for the sun to knock down

a thunderstorm
& then you hear
the kitchen clock

three score and ten years –
light at the end of
the bedroom hall

eternally
casting off earth
garden worm

pulling
one

bindweed
root

circum
navi

gate yr
world

SCOTT METZ

The moon and sun are eternal travelers. Even the years wander on. A lifetime adrift **in a boat**, or in old age leading a tired horse into the years, every day is a journey, and the journey itself is **home**. From the earliest times there have always been some who perished along the road. Still I have always been drawn by wind-**blown** clouds **into dreams** of a lifetime of wandering....

Translated by Sam Hamill
(*Narrow Road to the Interior and Other Writings*, 2000)

corp
orate
contami
nation

a whale
spouts

far off
shore

between my child and i
corporate language
disguised as a gull

        supermarket
         veteran

         pretends
        to shoot

          my
        daughter

         smiling

in the deep bosom
of a sniper –
myrtle blossom

狙撃兵のふところ深く百日紅
sogekihei no futokoro fukaku sarusuberi

hydrangea darkness –
the past gradually withers

あじさい闇　過去がどんどん痩せてゆく
ajisai yami kako ga dondon yasete yuku

Ōnishi Yasuyo
大西泰世

a machine gun
in the forehead
the killing flower blooms

機関銃眉間ニ殺ス花ガ咲ク
kikanjuu miken ni korosu hana ga saku
(1937)

Saitō Sanki
西東 三鬼

war
has stood
in the depth of the corridor

戦争が廊下の奥に立つてゐた
sensou ga rouka no oku ni tatte ita
(1939)

Watanabe Hakusen
渡辺白泉

a trench dug
to a depth of three feet –
death

塹壕の三尺の深さ堀りて死し
zangou no san-shaku no fukasa horite shishi

leaving a withered tree
being shot as a withered tree

枯れし木を離れ枯れし木として撃たれ
kareshi ki o hanare kareshi ki toshite utare

war dead
exit out of a blue mathematics

戦死者が青き数学より出たり
senshisha ga aoki suugaku yori detari
(1938)

Sugimura Seirinshi
杉村聖 林子

DIMITAR ANAKIEV

springtime in the state flag only three colors

MARLENE MOUNTAIN

a loss of content shapes painted over left to their own design

spin on dead and wounded any scratch of pines

bit by bit a bit on 'government secrecy'

computer crash as it falls snow reaches into my inner life

RICK TARQUINIO

blackout
some of the darkness
  is us

November wind
the garden reverts
to Latin

PETER MARCUS

Words at Dusk

The words I lost at dusk:
amulet, totem. If only to defy
the onslaught of the rust.

The aging of the airtight
mind. The verses made
of dust.
       Tomorrow is for
what? The autumnal sun
sinks beyond the stables

and the barns. The pasture
suddenly dimmer as if lit
by antique chandeliers.

My Tiny Miles Bible

How to know how
to compose a life?

Trumpet buried in the ground.
Trumpet buried in the sky.

So What is the score
for timelessness in time.

But for here
there is no heaven.

PETER NEWTON

How to Build a Birdhouse

Start with
a song

the one
you want

to hear.

Carry it
outside

and place it
out of reach.

sculpture park everything suspect

KIT KENNEDY

landscape, an unfinished conversation

tomorrow

undecipherable
damp napkin

MARKEITH CHAVOUS

shorthand
for a cloud
inside a blue jacket

SCOTT HONEYCUTT

Poem

A demon sits
knitting
in the corner
of all poetry.

ROB STANTON

Perverse

The 'i'
in 'subject'
is 'j'.

from *Sparks. Blinks*

Bored

salesgirl's

nametag reads,

'Hello: Infinity'

WES LEE

Trajectory

I can't wait to go home,
watch my serials, sink into
green velour and make a brew:

the glass coaster;
rocking to *True Crime*,
taking up where I left,

this place seems truer,
this place seems realer.

The office
where I sit for hours staring at a bullet
on its way to the skull.

Night Shift

Buildings –
silent like teeth
in a sleeping mouth.

DAVID BERRIDGE

into the field
beyond the street lamps
to let the moon rise
in the throat

RICHARD GILBERT

dedicated to the moon
i rise
without a decent alibi

three oceans
exported into orbit
in a small cocoon

Nothing Better

Basically, we saw nothing.
But we saw nothing better
than anyone else so far.*

Daniel McKinsey, particle physicist, wired.com

PETER HUGHES

I dreamed about the zenlessness of scaffolding
a universe full of light & airy cages
each one invisible

*

the ghostly assemblies of most of a lifetime
shimmer in midsummer dusk
faint blue July lines are converging behind us

*

so much of the earth is made of ruin compressed
into a temporary growing medium
fenced off & funded for a few baleful harvests

*

the river is illuminated by late light
echoing songs of redemption
though what is carried where remains a mystery

CHRISTOPHER PATCHEL

post-post-modernists expectant-ish

never enough horizon

once in a while a handful of harbour

GERALDINE MONK

from 'Poppyheads'

It was like the Mary Celeste except
we weren't at sea and no one was missing.
In a late summer night courtyard illuminated
shafts of wet creaked a simmering up-deep.

Moderation didn't make the
universe burst into pentameters.
Extremes teem. Petals and
thorns. Throne of frowns.

Dissembling blossoms
getting their peckers up for
autumnal crumble. Plum duff happens.
Lackadaisical bees – get well soon.

SHEILA E. MURPHY

how often
should I
refrain from watering
these weeds

vines I do not know the names of
challenge actuarial detail

treetop
small way
from the root

wash stones
wearing the rain

THOMAS A. CLARK

Afternoon

after sitting in thought
rise and go out
the colours saturated
leaves and grass wet

a breeze
of small birds
moving through
birch leaves

trembling of the leaves
trembling of the water
trembling of the light
thrown back by water

a ladder against
a quince tree
leading up into
leaves and fruit

BURT KIMMELMAN

Taking off from Orly Airport

> *'Out and back the mind'*
> – William Bronk

The city below,
the houses among

the mists of morning,
the stands of trees and

as we ascend the
wheat fields beyond them

all, the eye seeing
farther – we are just

as much there as here,
alien and true.

PETER YOVU

a drone widens the unpiloted blue

                              the second story
                              falls into the first   rubble
                              at the back of my throat

words furred over my awkward animal toward you now

so luscious
I forget
they're yours

after W.C.W.

turn there is
only the humming
bird's was

JOHN LEVY

(after Bashō)

My poems aren't
really mine. Any more

than a frog
owns its croak

or its splash as it dives
beneath the green surface.

You see the surface translated
into language

ripples. (The frog invisible,
immersed.)

Anguish

Sounds like something squashed, squished,
stepped on, lost.

An guish
rather than a guish, as if right off

you began wrong.

the crow inside the night inside the crow

for Cherie Hunter Day

Between Cages at the Zoo

3-year-old girl, alone,
stands on, and bends
over, the grated rain gutter

looks down into it

sticks
her fingers through

and shouts
into the darkness
Hi

lightning scrapes night's paint to salt

An IOU

'I owe you the truth in painting
and I shall tell it to you.'
– Cézanne

He gives us mountains of truth, the truth of color, the truth in jugs, in apples, the truth of a blue napkin, the truth snatched, the truth as this IOU, the truth of sunlight and the truth of white, the truth of a delicate practically impossible balance, different from the last almost impossible balance achieved. Parts and shards and bits of attention all over, intention and giving up at the same time.

WILLIAM CIROCCO

Les Oiseaux

mute stones
sang to
Brancusi
out of
their silence
birds flew

RACHEL CLOUD ADAMS

Giacometti

Down inside the thickening night,
the cicadas are contracting their muscle membranes,
and with the stacking of pattern upon pattern
they churn the air into a sound
as solid and attenuated
as the bronze insect waist of a Giacometti figure,
faceless, striding forward.

ROSMARIE WALDROP

At Color

if we look steadily
the eyes see white

    less is

if we then look at

another color
the eyes tend to subtract

    less than lest

that is, the
second color
moves
toward a kind
of indifference

    lest we go deep

BOB HEMAN

Perception

they went through
the wrong door
until their reason
became apparent

The Room

the room
they were given
full of animals
that never existed
full of names
for those animals
and the instructions
for their use

or a sudden hand
pulling the fields
from the earth &
making the sky
the angry ocean
it once was
when it used to talk
with men

there is only one night
that the days approach
to drink from

This street was a lot more interesting on the map.

CHERIE HUNTER DAY

bird's-eye view
torn wet and applied
to the appetite

sting medicine the lake's blue diction

moonlight the stitch in a metaphor

sleep handcuffed to a dimension

an ashen language in the drive-by of our bones

morphine fog for one

MARK HARRIS

Looking Back

Mom hasn't been all there, wherever there is, for a long time now. Slides like hers begin with bits of information lost, blanks we fill in moments later or not and move on. When did she slip away? A few years ago she told me, 'I'm losing my memory, you know, it's horrifying.' Her aspect was flat, her tone matter-of-fact. The situation brought to mind a Hiroshi Sugimoto photograph of a darkened movie theatre where he set up a camera loaded with black-and-white film, trained it on the screen, and opened the shutter for the duration of an entire movie. The beautiful architecture of the old theatre is faintly illumined by the screen. And the screen itself? All light, nothing but a glowing rectangle, what remains after every moving image is played out from beginning to end.

lack of a line
between ocean and sky –
scattered ashes

only a drawing
of a labyrinth, only
the moon's pull

EVE LUCKRING

what might suffice a peony's unfurled magnetic

a delta
of refrains
sun-scrubbed
salt
you who speak of clarity

ELIZABETH ROBINSON

On Terseness

Here's how I interrupted my story.

How I burnt my fingers on a match.

Here's how I scared the bears away from the garbage.

Underneath the great deluge there was nothing much.

It soaked up all that it could (story, fire, wild beast) but
    most of it

is surfeit, is not beholden to absorption, has fled within
    the bulk of itself.

MARK DuCHARME

Double

To still have captured what's not written
But *sounded*, in the space between breath &

Shadow. The event arrives
    Bearing its double –
An absent center
      Where the wind speaks

ANNA RECKIN

Clear Stories

I

lull,

    luck

ebb's pause

        stay

      where it listeth

II

    tied

       and lucent

sky-glad

        shrugs undone

III

islands reaching higher

    than trees

s'en fuient

   and the slow return

  aisle   *asile*   admittance

PETER ROBINSON

Coastal States

Given space, red sails in sunlight,
only pebbles on the beach
and people at true distances,
we're orientated, then let be;

we're ranged about West Wittering,
intimately diminished by
glints on rippling, moist expanses
before cloud-shadowed sea and sky.

Water Lights

Then it's you who points out how
a canoeing school flotilla
has dispersed the younger gulls
practising their killer
swoops and fishing dives.

Rippling over white-painted beams
of a seafood restaurant roof
are the low sun's wave reflections,
each thing as it seems.

LESLIE McGRATH

A Pinch

A smidgen, a speck, a trace, flung

... salt in the sweet dough
bitter in the savory ...

shadow taste, balance on the tongue

DAVID GIANNINI

A Jar

of black olives
shriveled in
brine – convo-

luted ruts to
the tongue:
each bitter

nipple an
odd Braille of
the withered

countryside
and the blind
pit within.

JOSEPH MASSEY

Hill's red
tethered
edge –

berries
that numbed
your tongue.

Eucalyptus
limbs lisp

wind winds
off the bay.

Swallows
whisk the rifts

dusk dims
between leaves

on the tree
whose name

I refuse to find.

MORRIS COX

from *45 Untitled Poems* (1969)

take
  pen
  ink
  paper

        what do you call this thing?
            it runs away

            open the door
          the wind enters

              write

among soft new leaves
a bird's black eye

upon fresh ringed water
a dotting of raindrops

with the wakening germ
a listening ear

things making words matching things

PAUL ROSSITER

Musica Universalis

we have	the spheres	the stars
an ear	ringing	singing
which can hear	in the frosty air	the winter of space

The Tramp

in the graveyard
said: Jesus

is coming soon
you know

I've only taken
to drink

as a temporary
measure

Attention

the railway workers
cross the line
stepping

casually
over one
live rail

(turning to
each other
and talking)

and then
the other – they
do this every

day, almost
not noticing
they're doing it

carefully

CHRIS BECKETT

Mallory in the Mountains

Left his compass at Camp V, his torch at Camp VI
inserted camera plates back to front
thought twice about oxygen

They found a broken
figure of uncertain direction
eaten by ravens.

Venice

Brackish lagoon, scarlet jasper.
Is war really possible without fantasy?
At the café, history tides

in translation. I drift across
the giddy surface of morning,
watching the arhythmic

pavement-tic
of impatient capital
impossible to disintricate.

STEPHANIE PAPA

Paris on Sunday

Every time the automatic doors
Start to close,
A drunk on the metro
Screams
Close the bloody doors
Then pries them back open
With his hands.

VICTORIA BEAN

Promised Land

I am off the drugs
oh yes,
I am off the drugs.

Celebration

A birthday drink.
A scrap in the street.

Break it up boys
but they just move further down the road
and do it again.

CHRIS McCABE

from 'Paternity Leave'

At ten pm, on his fifth day, a syringe of antibiotics

– precautionary, for the black owl of the kidney –

The Blue Planet, somewhere out there, in digital, soothes –

amniotic, hypnotic –

as if Attenborough is our paymaster –

the hatchlings, however, have already started out on their journey

JANE MONSON

The sky turns cartoon
birds fall into clouds, laughing:
death can't touch us here

JESSE GLASS

from 'Museum'

Roman sarcophagus

women carved on it

one seated
        face in hands

others playing

        timbrels

        pipes.

translated: 'for
  the shade of
  Galatia Vitalis
  aged 16 years
  when death took
  her. dark
  gods of the under
  world treat her
  well.'

  chiseled leaves

carved thrysi

boxes filled
with shattered bones
    'sacred to Proserpine'

unguents
        poured
by traces
of an arm.

stone

mirror
fogged with
breath
of

stone.

GARY HOTHAM

bare floor
around the stain –
an old month on the calendar

over the give away table
clouds that don't need
a wind

light
that's left
for light that's left

anxious morning
daylight staying out of
the rocks

more stone
inside the stone –
child's play

GEORGE SWEDE

our backyard trees –
their unconditional
unconcern

self-scrutiny
the murky pond
amputating sunbeams

high tide
thoughts without brains
shimmer in moonlight

high tide
my OCD splintering
on the sea wall

HELEN BUCKINGHAM

daybreak
blackdog
pixelating

emergency space walk …
I brace myself
to leave the house

anonymous arterial … humanity-sprayed walls

art school
fixing
the urinal

ALISTAIR NOON

from 'Station and Street'

Let the green sweepings increase into a pile
with each push of the broom from your dungareed knees,
servant of the platform's trodden concrete and tiles:
the floors of Delphi never gleamed like these.

Landlord

Could your hobby be the study of fungi
that live in the crevices of tree trunks,
their threads extracting the nutrients,
their caps a portfolio of spores?

You took away my seas, the run and the running jump,
and brought my toes to rest on the earth now violated,
achieving what? Yes, brilliant the way you settled up:
lips that won't stop twitching can't be amputated.

(Osip Mandelstam, *May* 1935)

Reading Kafka

```
ka ka
   f
ka ka
   f
   f ka
ka f
   fka
kaf
  a a
   f
  a a
   f
   f a
 a f
   fa
 af
 afa
 a fa
  af a
 Kafka
```

On Trial

A hand's on trial for the body, but the body says the mind's charged with criminal acts and the hand, merely an accomplice. Who gets off and who asks? The body's a pulse-code of beats and abdominal rumblings while the mind is figuring. Look closely at the boundary, in and out. If you're lucky, it disappears and it's not a game of cat and mouse.

LARISSA SHMAILO

I am not your insect

Your underfoot, your exterminated, your bug. My un-
abashedly hairy legs, whose gymnopédies twitch like a
chorus for a fatal Sharon Stone, delight in *ces mouvements
qui déplace les lignes*, in the motion, the quiver, *le mort*, the
catch. Mother Kali, you have made me what I am: feminine,
brilliant, entirely without fear. Like my mother, I watch and
pray for prey – that it be there, that it give gore, that I feel it
die, that there be more.

JOHN M. BENNETT

Sog

the long fog the dancing
whiff the blam hog the
glancing roar the ham dog
the rancid elf the glans
log the stammered hip the
grease bog the antsy drip
the wrong cog the massif

ROBERT SHEPPARD

hammerhead

ughhuh ha
drum tick
slivery gl
iss-squeez

ed (s)crea
m voc-vol
trat-ahhhh
-yaya thum

punked hic
suck upsh
ivery glik

shot out o
f throaty
tub-thramp

(track 12, john zorn's *naked city* cd, 1989)

ROBERT HAMPSON

from 'the war against tourism'

lifts the flap on the buckle
the new world disorder
or the law of unintended consequences
the occupying army controls
only what it can shoot
pull the mask towards you
already you begin to lose
the borders of your identity
pull it over your head
how do you locate yourself
take up the protective brace position
with both feet flat on the floor
& 24,000 feet beneath you
we'll know where to find your teeth

JEFF HARRISON

Swedenborg exploded,
& also certain angels

JOEL CHACE

from 'Heaveng'

1

Between Lewis's 'it would have to be

the biggest hoax ever perpetrated'

       and the holy, blank scrolls that Monkey finds

       you could drive a starship

Beelzebub tells tales within the dead body of his spacecraft

2

Could weariness really be the point? *Bien sur.*

No height; no width; no depth; no color:

       all the mad purpose of a mad universe.

Which you can write down but probably shouldn't say aloud

PHILIP TERRY

from 'Homage To Catatonia'
Mistranslations from the Catalan of Agusti Bartra

VII
Look at your conscience.
The syntax of usury:
White geraniums!

XVI
If not the flags, then
The mute pollen of the sun.
Begin to listen.

XXIV
Decanting the hours
He creates a bronze torso
With a mouth of wool.

XXVI
Hand signals begin
When lip movements grow obscure:
End of the earth.

XXVII
The pitiless force
Of the death factories.
Does it excite you?

XXVIII
Impalpable father,
Teaching the art of loss, and
Campanology.

XLV
No one can explain
The enigma of the cats
Hanging from the trees.

LII
The message hovers
Between chaos and dialogue.
Loom at its centre.

LVIII
The poet. The man.
Be one who flies from neither.
Stress management.

Larkin Paraphrased

Your mother and father cause you permanent psychological damage. They probably do this inadvertently. They pass all the defects they inherited on to you, as well as some additional ones they manufacture uniquely for your benefit. But their mothers and fathers, dressed in old-fashioned clothes, caused them permanent psychological damage in their turn, with violent mood swings from the stiffly sentimental to the confrontational. Unhappiness is passed on from one generation to the next. It increases in depth like the tidal erosion of the offshore sea bed. My advice is to participate in this cycle as little as is humanly possible, by avoiding acts of procreation.

TADPOLES

❦

❦ ❦

❦ ❦ ❦ ❦ ❦

❦ ❦ ❦ ❦ ❦ ❦ ❦ ❦

❦ ❦ ❦ ❦ ❦ ❦ ❦ ❦

❦ ❦ ❦ ❦ ❦ ❦ ❦ ❦

❦ ❦ ❦ ❦ ❦ ❦ ❦

❦ ❦ ❦ ❦ ❦ ❦ ❦ ❦ ❦

❦ ❦ ❦ ❦

❦ ❦ ❦ ❦ ❦ ❦ ❦ ❦

❦ ❦ ❦ ❦ ❦ ❦ ❦ ❦

❦ ❦ ❦ ❦ ❦ ❦ ❦ ❦ ❦

❦ ❦ ❦ ❦ ❦ ❦ ❦ ❦ ❦ ❦

❦ ❦ ❦ ❦ ❦ ❦ ❦ ❦ ❦

❦ ❦ ❦ ❦ ❦ ❦ ❦

FROGS

f
r   p
p o o l
g   o
    p

Six Degrees of Continuous Disclosure

It is important
to differentiate

between a
good metaphor

& an asteroid
that has ripened.

Sorry,

nothing
matched your
search terms. Please

try again with
a different
fish.

CHRIS GORDON

a love letter to the butterfly gods with strategic misspellings

all the ceiling fans moving at different speeds

JIM KACIAN

Sonnet
for
Philip
Glass

sturmsturmsturmsturmsturmsturmsturmsturmsturmsturm
stormstormstormstormstormstormstormstormstormstorm
storestorestorestorestorestorestorestorestorestore
stonestonestonestonestonestonestonestonestonestone
sconesconesconesconesconesconesconesconesconescone
scenescenescenescenescenescenescenescenescenescene
scentscentscentscentscentscentscentscentscentscent
scantscantscantscantscantscantscantscantscantscant
slantslantslantslantslantslantslantslantslantslant
plantplantplantplantplantplantplantplantplantplant
plankplankplankplankplankplankplankplankplankplank
prankprankprankprankprankprankprankprankprankprank
drankdrankdrankdrankdrankdrankdrankdrankdrankdrank
drangdrangdrangdrangdrangdrangdrangdrangdrangdrang

in a tent in the rain i become a climate

another day in paradise lost in translation

at the end of the sordid life some beautiful illness

all the links go somewhere paranoid

one thought over
laps another un
til both are gone

BARRY SCHWABSKY

Cartesian Medication

No mind
no body
no problem.

Polonaise Fantaisie

Strange gestures of musicians. The way a pianist might draw
a hand up with resolve, as if to entice some weighty chord to
linger in the air just that much longer, or even haul a stray
note bodily from the abyss of the keyboard as one would a
child that has tumbled into the well. What bothers me is
how this useless coaxing sometimes seems to work.

Three Threes for Lee Harwood

Orphan lines
Of verse in your wallet:
Ideal currency.

Two dark birds hover
Overcast sky hangs low
Past the clouds – who knows?

Pleasure spun backwards:
Words stick to your fingers
You lick them slowly.

ALAN HALSEY

Ars Poetica

for Alec Finlay

The sayable
   in nouns
in syllables
   is nuance

As if a flock
   of small birds ate
the feeder but
   left the nuts

Fragments Doubtfully Ascribed To Mercurialis The Younger

neither flavour of vinegar nor fervour of winejar

*

for writing your speeches, Fabius, how was I rewarded?
– with an official invitation to Simonidize the war-dead

*

stranger, if you sniff something acrid
in the air here – these were the many-acred
fields of Saturnus the banker who'd
always said there was nothing sacred

from *Lives of the Poets*

Matthew Green

my well-meant joco-serious song
From Peter Drake to Stephen Duck
When I came to London
What course and want of method I took
Tarantulated and Phylacter'd
to drive away that spectre Spleen

William Lisle Bowles

Bowles who never comes amiss
Moore says
His sheep bells are tuned in thirds and fifths

William Hone

if an intention were good I took a pair of scissors
(for that is the way I make books)
with my friend Cruikshank in my hall of Parody
send me up my tea and the House that Jack built
There is not one line I would blot

CAROL WATTS

John Clare

called
them
pigions
he
frit
the
lark
up
while
raking
so
ryhmd
on
and
became
pacified

SUSAN DIRIDONI

under a wheelbarrow a snake absorbing grace

roses clamber over your daunting fatigue

latitude far north confounding sun slants

PATRICK DONNELLY
        AND STEPHEN MILLER (translators)

He wrote this longing for the paradise in the West

though I've heard
            the distance to supreme delight
                is vast
                        with practice
            I can reach that place
by morning

                            — Priest Senkei
Shūishū 1343

極楽は遥けきほどと聞きしかどつとめて至る所なりけり

gokuraku wa   harukeki hodo to   kikishikado   tsutomete itaru
tokoro narikeri

Five hundred disciples receive the prophecy that
they will attain Buddhahood

of the jewel
sewn in my coat

    I had no inkling

what luck!
to wake

    from my long drunkenness

          – Akazome Emon
Goshūishū 1194

ころもなる玉ともかけて知らざりき酔ひさめてこそうれしかりけれ

koromo naru   tama to mo kakete   shirazariki   eisamete koso
ureshikarikere

CARRIE ETTER

The Love Plot

after Ono no Komachi

In bliss you spill words
richly implicit, diamonds
I fear will not cut glass
come morning and all
the armoury of reason.

First Summer

Children swing from bar to bar as we pass. Once the path has
delivered us through a dense stand of poplars, their calls must
be imagined.

On this side of the trees, an overgrown meadow spills away
from town. If we break the weeds with our bodies, your
downward gaze displaces the sky.

We leave with the strip of forest at our backs. Now the children
will play forever, turning a roundabout under the moon.

The Crucible, Sheffield

Watching the snooker world championship on TV, the
    defending
champion   career as a verb   body and mind in concert
and the challenger two frames ahead   watch in and out of
    thought
the song mere murmur amid   bright attention bright
    otherness
at that angle   using the spider   terrific pot
selves shed to one or unify in the act of concentration
behind the red   at what consequence

       twilit tide pool –
       a hermit crab wriggles
       into a new shell

AIDAN SEMMENS

overwintering dunlin spatter the mud
intent as mites on cheese

from small deliverances
the passengers arrive
clutching their lovely things

the hunt for unclaimed bones
beneath a helicopter sky

a child's fur-grimed toy
snared in a hedge

BOYER RICKEL

Shame

Wrapped inside a newspaper, behind a brick in the chimney,
a canary inside a frayed blue purse inside a can.

A continual performance.

Love igniting that place in the caudate nucleus.

The day so searing, when walking from sunlight into the
shade of a palo verde, I felt the cool glide up my shins as
though I'd stepped into a pool of water.

The ghost had died, returning as a body.

Forgiveness

The problem of infinities.

Spanning the beach, decayed gradations, one gull so freshly dead it seemed a toe might nudge it into flight, the next a dreary hump, mere moldered feathers, and then a heap of bones, a necklace cast aside with one long golden pendant, and so on.

A ladder, each rung the future of the rung below, until nothing.

A buoyant emptiness.

The smell of just-sprayed sidewalks before the start of business.

BOB ARNOLD

Sidewalk

Such a
Beautiful woman

Really, I couldn't
Take my eyes off

Her, slow with
Her age in the

Rain, wearing
A perfectly made

Newspaper
Pirate hat

Dawn

To live by a woods river
Forever is to finally
Forget it

& to remember
It again
Is something

JONATHAN GREENE

As It Was

The bullfrogs
guard me

from the noise
of modern life

the stars
fool me into

thinking they always
look the same.

JOHN PHILLIPS

Identity

No, I was never there.

That was someone else
who recalls
meeting you
in a place
neither of us
ever visited.

Remember?

Recognition

Towards five
in the morning:
My hand creates
the words
I write,
the words I write
create me.

Day breaks in my body.

moon
on
water

no
closer

Mont St. Victoire

The hand painting
   the mountain
      creates the mountain
    we go to
     see

JIM MOORE

The young woman on the train

uses as a bookmark
        a postcard of the Mona Lisa.
She sleeps, while in the distant field
        at the edge of the painting
just poking up through her book
        I see the light da Vinci loved,
the blue light of ambulances at night
        when they pulse out their warnings.

*

It may be that dying

is a little like leaving Venice:
        all this confusion
and worry about catching a train
        that is only going to Bologna.

LEE GURGA

we
linger
at
breakfast
mother's burial dress
on
a
hanger
in
the
car

ROBERTA BEARY

day moon –
we windowshop
caskets

SABINE MILLER

My Life Behind Glass

so lonely, the little verbs

ELEANOR STANFORD

Domestic

She snaps the linens square.
A field of flax: glaucous green,
slender lanceolate,
unspun. She crossed the border
lying on a raft. Perhaps
her eyes were shut. Perhaps
staring at the muddy sky.

EMILY CARR

sunset flings blood & taffeta across the crumbling sill she is
frankly unemployable –

        dandelion to the
        instant, a
        sparrow empties
        its cry into the
        blank memory
        of heaven *the*
        Lord, a billboard
        says, *is my*
        shepherd [I shall
        not want]

            after R. Armantrout

RUTH DANON

Warning

Message from a room
formerly filled
with light:

Nothing prepared me
for inquisition
or pilgrimage. Not
cold stones, not bare feet.

mole of moonlight

      scrubber of dreams, paws

in the half light scrape at the

      dirt

what tales

      you will tell

when the spilt milk

      pools in the rock

DIETMAR TAUCHNER

man-made lake
swimming in
our own imaginations

snow in the creator's synapses

RICHARD KOSTELANETZ

S**NO**W

NICK RAVO

⌐

AX

Robert Lax (In Memoriam)

SANDRA SIMPSON

the last sister
escorted to a front pew –
dandelion lawn

end of the month –
the clatter of a knife
in an empty jar

menopause
a swan hisses
dementedly

Act IV when the winter crow recognizes me

counterclockwise wars of my father

RUTH LEPSON

Function Theory

To the left of zero
and into the center
of negative numbers
to imaginary ones
where beauty   doesn't
imply exclusion.
The square root
of a negative
number, thought
forms of a little girl.

MARK E. BRAGER

late winter crows skirting the last digit of pi

MARK TERRILL

A road crosses a road another road does not.

PHILIP ROWLAND

from 'Bio Notes'

puddled night pavement –
the shape my past
refuses to take

*

measured for a burial:
the distance from
self to word

*

He was trying (they may say)
to say something, but was
too busy chewing on something
mistaken for nothingness.

RUFO QUINTAVALLE

Static

In half-lit rooms a radio tuned to nothing buzzes static,
a burr like the music of history,

which explains nothing
but without which we cannot explain;

it is this sound not silence we wake and sleep to
and by it know we are the same that wake who slept.

DANIEL ZIMMERMAN

Quantum Mechanics

nothing keeps happening.
poetry still works.

GLORIA FRYM

Please Understand

there was no story

                          no arc of triumph

       don't be disappointed
       think lyrically

                  with a photograph

there'd be proof
       balk all you like   things moved

                         around even

       forward not this

JANE HIRSHFIELD

Everything Has Two Endings

Everything has two endings –
a horse, a piece of string, a phone call.

Before a life, air.
And after.

As silence is not silence, but a limit of hearing.

CONTRIBUTORS

AUTHORS' BOOKS

Some of the poems first published in NOON: *journal of the short poem* and included in this anthology later appeared, or will soon appear, in the following books:

Rachel Cloud Adams: *Space and Road* (Semiperfect Press, 2019).

Victoria Bean: *Caught* (Smokestack Books, 2011).

Helen Buckingham: *sanguinella* (Red Moon Press, 2017).

Ruth Danon: *Word Has It* (Nirala Series, 2018).

Cherie Hunter Day: *for Want* (Ornithopter Press, 2017), *sting medicine* (e-book, *Bones: journal for contemporary haiku*, 2016).

Alan Halsey: *Not Everything Remotely* (Salt Publishing, 2005), *Lives of the Poets* (Five Seasons Press, 2009), *Selected Poems 1988-2016* (Shearsman Books, 2017).

Robert Hampson: *reworked disasters* (Knives Forks And Spoons Press, 2013).

Bob Heman: *Assuming the Light, As If, seven structures* (self-published pamphlets).

Gary Hotham: *Stone's Throw: Promises of Mere Words* (Pinyon Publishing, 2016).

Jane Hirshfield: *Come, Thief* (Knopf, 2011 and Bloodaxe Books, 2011).

Jim Kacian: *after/image* (Red Moon Press, 2017).

Elmedin Kadric: *buying time* (Red Moon Press, 2017).

Burt Kimmelman: *Abandoned Angel: New Poems* (Marsh Hawk Press, 2016).

Ruth Lepson: *I Went Looking for You* (blazeVOX, 2009).

John Levy: *Oblivion, Tyrants, Crumbs* (First Intensity Press, 2008). *In the Pit of the Empty* (e-book, otata's bookshelf, 2017), *On Its Edge, Tilted* (e-book, otata's bookshelf, 2018).

Joseph Massey: *Areas of Fog* (Shearsman Books, 2009)

Chris McCabe: *THE RESTRUCTURE* (Salt Publishing, 2012).

Geraldine Monk: *Lobe Scarps and Finials* (Leafe Press, 2011).

Jim Moore: *Invisible Strings* (Graywolf Press, 2011).

Peter Newton: *The Searchable World* (Mapleview Publishing, 2017).

Alistair Noon: *Swamp Area* (Longbarrow Press, 2012), *Concert at a Railway Station: Selected Poems* of Osip Mandelstam (Shearsman Books, 2018).

John Phillips: *Shape of Faith* (Shearsman Books, 2017), *Heretic* (Longhouse Publishers & Booksellers, 2016).

Rufo Quintavalle: *Make Nothing Happen* (Oystercatcher Press, 2009); *Weather Derivatives* (Eyewear Publishing, 2014).

Boyer Rickel: *remanence* (Parlor Press, 2009).

Peter Robinson: *Collected Poems* 1976-2016 (Shearsman Books, 2017).

Paul Rossiter: *Seeing Sights* (Isobar Press, 2016), *Temporary Measures* (Isobar Press, 2017).

Philip Rowland: *Something Other Than Other* (Isobar Press, 2016).

Barry Schwabsky: *Trembling Hand Equilibrium* (Black Square Editions, 2015).

Larissa Shmailo: *#specialcharacters* (Unlikely Books, 2014).

Eleanor Stanford: *Bartram's Garden* (Carnegie Mellon Press, 2015).

Rick Tarquinio: *star by star* (Odd Duck Press, 2017).

Michelle Tennison: *murmuration* (Red Moon Press, 2016).

Philip Terry: *Oulipoems* (Ahadada, 2007), *Oulipoems* 2 (Ahadada, 2009).

Rosmarie Waldrop: *Splitting Image* (Zasterle Books, 2005).

Mark Young: *some more strange meteorites* (Meritage Press and i.e. press, 2017), *Bricolage* (gradient books, 2017), *the eclectic world* (gradient books, 2014).